Reading Partners

by Michèle Dufresne

Pioneer Valley Educational Press, Inc.

I am reading to the monkey.

I am reading to the dog.

I am reading to the dinosaur.

I am reading to the bear.

I am reading to the frog.

I am reading to the lion.

I am reading to the turtle.

I am reading to my friend.